FROM DEEP SPACE YOU CANNOT HEAR
WHAT WE SAY

FROM DEEP SPACE YOU CANNOT HEAR WHAT WE SAY

poems
David Blumel

TALL ISLAND PRESS
New York, New York

Copyright © 2023 by David Blumel
Cover image © Tall Island Press
All Rights Reserved.

FIRST EDITION

This book is a work of fiction. All the names, characters, businesses, places, events, and incidents in this book are used fictitiously.

Tall Island Press
New York, NY 10013

For permission to use the contents, please contact tallislandpress@gmail.com.

ISBN-10: 0991327217
ISBN-13: 978-0991327218
Library of Congress Control Number: 2023917043

for y'all

CONTENTS

1 Into the Unknown
2 System Sound
3 Footsteps
4 Post to Chain
5 Moonshot Blast Off
6 Rambling On
7 Y'all Confused
8 Breakfast Is Coming
9 New Year's Reservations
10 Coffee Shop
11 Hand-Painted
12 Estimates Predicted the Opposite
13 In Symmetrical Cases
14 A Story of Life
15 Restoration
16 The Remedy
17 Fruitless but Passable
18 Cast Tentacles of a Messy Theory
19 A Modulated Dose
20 The Diagnosis Took Time
21 Warped
22 Fusion Line
23 Betting That It Costs Less
24 Together
25 Water-Flower-Ripen Approach
26 Almost Everything Looks Important
27 Determination
28 Tidying Up the Edges
29 A Barrel of Technology
30 Where Your Dreams Are Paid

31 Mystics, Facies and Piffle
32 Back Struts
33 Recognizing Mistakes
34 Stop Recording
35 Into the Wood
36 Stick to the Be That
37 And Them Noises
38 But No
39 Relational Instability
40 In Fact, We Promise
41 A Distinct Vision
42 Bash Street
43 Asked and Found
44 Cha-Cha Betcha
45 Travel
46 Overcook Out
47 Inflating Your Currency
48 Roots Underfoot
49 Trace Track
50 Friday Night

FROM DEEP SPACE YOU CANNOT HEAR
WHAT WE SAY

INTO THE UNKNOWN

Wandering, we were surrounded
by distant figures
borne along the miles

to where the past
presses forward
in gravitational bursts

followed by more seasonal weather
as predicted
evoking memories

of moments of happiness
in moonlit spots
enraptured.

SYSTEM SOUND

Tightening your grip
energized the chamber

equalizing the system
and filling the passage

with breath on all sides
in colors and in pieces

which developed
until absorbed by the receiver.

FOOTSTEPS

Having traversed
twenty-three uninhabited islands
our plan seemed to stall.

Moving the fence
would have speeded the excavation
of our collective undoing.

POST TO CHAIN

Immortality being unusual
rather than reminiscence

E spoke convincingly
of an intersecting curve

related in structural agreement
to a road crossing a canal.

MOONSHOT BLAST OFF

You entered the solar frontier
quietly

as a biologic speck
with less gravity than usual.

Backtracking, you observed
a sweet, icy silence

and spotted your shadow
drop-twisting away.

RAMBLING ON
(A CITY WALK)

As you weeded, hoed and plowed
your way downtown

lacy curls
hung like fragile signs

above your eyes
framing worry lines.

Five kilometers and a few trees later
you encountered the fury of lava

flowing faster than
a blinking light bulb.

Sensing the usual belly-creeping dangers
and a few other nerve-tingling trends

hands in pockets
you pressed on.

Y'ALL CONFUSED

We dug out hard-to-grow
stumpy forest species
symbolizing
spare matter
evolution
and quiet discord
all presented in green.

BREAKFAST IS COMING

Beyond the minimum time for fun
a particular hang-up-belief, or not

S discovered that
laughter will be earlier this month.

Stepping in the way of reason
did slow her down.

It was just the way she moved
and how her inspirations worked.

Socially trained
in style and comfort

the position of her teeth
were straight from Hollywood.

NEW YEAR'S RESERVATIONS

Waves of excitement
overlapping

aggressively rang
your consciousness.

As the night's last stitch closed
booming thunder

made you stand
spoon up, clock and glare.

COFFEE SHOP

Before I sat down
it began to register

that the continuity of the grid
had started sinking.

Expansive schematizing
of the interspaced tiles

mercifully improved my perception
of the animals who cling to us.

But that's how puppies are.

HAND-PAINTED

Color tones
may change very quickly
depending on scalular conditions.

Cool, metallic blue tones
are very rare
in background noise.

The right arrow control
has greatly improved their intonation.
Their strength seems brighter, too.

Raspberry is a cheery tone.

ESTIMATES PREDICTED THE OPPOSITE

The enemy is a ceramic structure
stranded, with receding form
and connected
by a nanothread
to a revolt
in your backyard.

Harmony
is similarity encaged
and varies with time
like a repeat sniffle
detuned
and unzipped.

IN SYMMETRICAL CASES

A proof-supported adjustment
inserted into the code

cleanly repaired
the fault-line damage

as a small speaker
broadcast

over-released
feel-good lyrics

wrapped up, and cemented in
making time disappear

with simulated side effects
squashed.

A STORY OF LIFE

The line extended
point-by-point
and penetrated
ply-by-ply.

Broken into segments
the line slowly disintegrated
and forgotten boundaries
expanded.

RESTORATION

A well-defined
sensory pathway

charged at the entrance
led to a stimulus

whose heavy foundation
without warning

acknowledged reincarnation
and transformed itself.

THE REMEDY

By force, luck
or the law of efficiency

shaking loose from the scars
sticking to you

freed you like a falling tide
liberates the sea

allowing your fire to rise to levels
close to those of a raging river.

FRUITLESS BUT PASSABLE

Heavily alarmed, and rightfully disclosed
specimens
appeared to be docking.

Protecting their temperament
involved automatic
decoupling of the system.

The chosen strategy
hinted at hard-to-remember
but inspiring concepts.

Rearranging the calendar
you wondered, what if
what if occurred?

CAST TENTACLES OF A MESSY THEORY

Chasing the experience
of an attractively dreamt story

N whooped a roaring rush of notes
impetuously connected

in the spirit
of flute and fiddle

and compressed into sharp
disjointed forms

blazing
and spread asunder.

A MODULATED DOSE

A mouthful of jello
incrementally warmed up

and microphysically cleaved
produced a soft fascination.

THE DIAGNOSIS TOOK TIME

The revolving room
is unwieldy and distorted.

Steadying
and assessing my balance

it occurred to me
that the movement

could be considered
basking in time

warming everything
touched.

WARPED

Wistfully withstanding
the amplified state

and grim beauty
of a punk scream

I exited and stumbled upon
a million surprises

some, clear shockers
and others, quite familiar.

FUSION LINE

Super-stuffed
with grass fabric

and drawing fearlessly
you indulged

in a calculated path
to fly the violet sky.

BETTING THAT IT COSTS LESS

Even when applying thick paint
hopes
can be fooled.

Still, genetically engineered fixes
expressed as ecstatic allusions
nailed behind

astrobiological artifacts
will calm jumpy vibrations
and stop you in your tracks.

TOGETHER

As one of a couple
of wonders

life's metallic shield
is a sleek, reflective

coat
with key dimensions

connecting impulses
spiraling along

logistic pathways
inhabiting all.

WATER-FLOWER-RIPEN APPROACH

For spare-part advocacy
you tried fishing

for relics
of a classic look

to produce a static hiss
along a sequenced channel

toward a balanced wave
between storms

end or shine.

ALMOST EVERYTHING
LOOKS IMPORTANT

Your brain
is a loosely wound

sphere
of chemical medicine

inside of which
the comedy

unfolds.

DETERMINATION

In the interval between the door
and the horse shed

you substituted one fixation
for another

that had considerable mind disruption
wired in parallel.

TIDYING UP THE EDGES

Early morning, an obstacle whose shape
clearly possessed magnificence
ate at our confidence.

Toward the opposite end of the day
circumstances differed
because of cloud openings.

By evening, the starry sky
supported
feel-good emotions

causing our heartbeats to spill out
effortlessly
and become fluid.

A BARREL OF TECHNOLOGY

Appraising the value
of the routine function
within the operation
you cut the balky connection
and firmly balanced
the task.

Sheared luminous rays
boosted the effect
and light-wave communication
enabled the update
to the robot's
self-driving clunker.

WHERE YOUR DREAMS ARE PAID

The construction was
a curlicue

a feat
swirling and sleek

presenting a ticklish turn
from a dazzling plan

circumferentially sweeping
loosely speaking.

MYSTICS, FACIES AND PIFFLE

An all-night
project popped.

Stone after stone
you extended.

In a daring exchange
B clasped your shoulder.

You reciprocated
by whispering distractions.

You tried to guess
and kept on guessing.

BACK STRUTS

A gnarly pattern
of bongo notes

drummed offbeat
ripped crystal clear

through the night air
with heavy-handed

accents
sonically wrinkled.

RECOGNIZING MISTAKES DEVELOPING TRADE-OFFS AND CLAIMING AUTONOMY

Whimsical emotions
of perceptual importance
drawn from pop fairy tales
dangled in the balmy air.

Sandwiched between
a major bobble
and a minor detachment
you waltzed and swayed.

Released from all constraints
you drove confidently
radar beams on
avoiding endangered species.

STOP RECORDING

A coat of green
a spot of black
and a rose streak
were more than I could stand.

Despite the neural chaos
upending my witchy balance
to feed the thrill
V painted her toenails radish purple.

Tuning the wavelengths
by a few nanometers
I felt connected to the continuum
and bowed to the jumpy fuss.

INTO THE WOOD

Borer, prowler, pest
barbaric sap straw

impaling pine stock
tunneling ash

and festering *Ulmus* ruins
until wrung dry.

STICK TO THE BE THAT

The weight of my worry
in kilotons

hinged on
the problem of icky mathematics

the repetitive kind
of body-at-rest nonsense

that kept destiny afloat
until the Big Bang.

AND THEM NOISES

The swarm, moving faster
formed a looping pattern

fast and wide
pulsating

before stabilizing
on common ground

as you stood silent
perplexed.

BUT NO

I am not a wrap wedge clip zipper
which is an old stopper

embedded in concrete
and rewired finger to joint.

RELATIONAL INSTABILITY

In the preparation of dirt
you held your ground.

Lying low, you slipped around
to avoid the blur, the severe

myopic division of things
as onlookers noticed at length

that the mask
had lost its eyelashes.

IN FACT, WE PROMISE

Anyone can quickly forget about
just how seemingly exactly

seemingly exactly can be
such as the fluidity of the sea

with its bobbing life
salt and whales.

A DISTINCT VISION

Oh black-tea box
foretasting your mystery

I sensed a feeling
(quirky, all in all)

of holding the reins
tight

and a willingness
to yawn.

BASH STREET

Feasting on mangled vegetation,
siphoning the blurry loose ends
of pungent organics

and expressing pleasantly tight
meandering emotions
produced a squishy effect

with excellent suction
that smoothly decayed
and sparked your curiosity.

ASKED AND FOUND

Making a case for something you own
and had doubts about
but kept anyway

you asked two people with stomachaches
about the plan
who said it was a matter of taste.

CHA-CHA BETCHA

Theorizing about a shift
in a transition state

corresponding to a steep
and powerful thermal transfer

from your skin
to one eye and couple of teeth

you rose to dance
amid the glittering stars.

TRAVEL
(or just a meaningless ambition to go)

Deep fried by infrared radiation
and dynamically loaded
with internal fancy

you traveled via riderless horse
thru extension of simulating
sustainable sympathy.

OVERCOOK OUT

Trying to hide your blush
created a conspicuous
glow behind you

and induced a positive coupling
of feedback loops
that gelled to great irony.

In response to sensations
neither dogmatic nor spiritual
but completely physical

you ran at a tumultuous pace
causing your body language
to link to a down-shifting bus.

INFLATING YOUR CURRENCY

Gently shaking the ground
where the sky hits the plains

exposed everything
the people, the scene.

I can't imagine what you've gotten into
protecting what was crumbling

mending old walls
and pruning tall trees.

Your currency has worn splendidly
but the cost has been debated.

ROOTS UNDERFOOT

Feeling a sudden urge
to be on your feet

you set off
into the summer sun

and followed the stairs
to a familiar path, where

weighing a heavily rooted theory
you chose a countermeasure

based on a familiar influence
and made a plan

to write about
the science of silence.

TRACE TRACK

Being a skilled skeptic, you questioned
whether the abundance of settling dust
had educatory promise.

Tightening up their ragged-edged curves
strengthened the overlapping dust layers
creating a sedimentary boundary.

Standing on the fringes
you let your hair down to fall in line
with the stability you observed.

FRIDAY NIGHT

As happy as we were
it was time to forget
the story that so-captivated us.

Stirring with hope in a new reality
we linked to the source
and switched it on.

From the pitch and the catch
we eventually got used to
the purple growl.

Sooner or later
the rules
could go under the bridge.

Tonight we are managing.
But from deep space
you cannot hear what we say.

www.ingramcontent.com/pod-product-compliance
Lightning Source LLC
Chambersburg PA
CBHW030458010526
44118CB00011B/992